Some Nights I Flip My Lid

Learning To Be a Calm, Cool Kid

Kellie Doyle Bailey, MA CCC-SLP, MMT/SELI

Illustrated by **Hannah Bailey**

Some Nights I Flip My Lid
Copyright © 2020 Kellie Doyle Bailey

Published by:
PESI Publishing & Media, Inc.
3839 White Ave.
Eau Claire, WI 54703

Illustrations: Hannah Bailey
Cover: Hannah Bailey
Layout: Amy Rubenzer

ISBN: 9781683733577

Library of Congress Control Number: 2020946379

Printed in Canada

My name is Grace
and I am nine.

I'm in the 4th grade
and some days are fine.

On days that are fine I can hear and see all the great things my teachers show me.

I have a best friend,
her name is Maysie.

We love reading,
math, art, and PE.

Maysie and I have other friends too, and together we have lots of fun at school.

Some days are easy, I like those the best because I'm **CALM** in my body, my brain, and my chest.

On easy days, my learning is fun. I can pay attention on purpose and get lots of things done.

On easy days, I feel **CALM** and **COOL**, and most of the time I'm okay in school.

But then there are days when there's too much to do or my teacher is out and the substitute's new.

These are the days when it's tricky for me
to **LISTEN** and **LEARN**, to **HEAR**, and to **SEE**.

These are the days when I feel lots of **STRESS**.
My learning just **STOPS**, and I can't do my best.

STRESS is a feeling that starts in
my mind, and it lives in my heart
and slides down my spine.

On **STRESSFUL** days, my learning's not fun.

On **STRESSFUL** days, I just want to run.

I don't ever run, I stay stuck in my seat.

I feel **ANXIOUS** and **STRESSED** from my head to my feet.

I just wish people would **LEAVE ME ALONE.**

I really wish that I could **GO HOME.**

Are you ever **STRESSED?**

Do you want to **GO HOME?**

Do you ever wish people would **LEAVE YOU ALONE?**

And then there are days when I'm **ANXIOUS** or **SAD.**

I had a **FIGHT** with my friend and now I feel **BAD.**

These are the days when I don't feel okay.

I just want to **FLY** far, far away.

But I don't **FLY** away.

I see the nurse instead because...**WORRY** is stuck in my heart and my head.

Are you ever **WORRIED?**

Do you want to **GO HOME?**

Do you ever wish people would **LEAVE YOU ALONE?**

And then there are days when I'm **EMBARRASSED** and **ASHAMED.**

I struck out in kickball, and my team lost the game.

These are the days when I just want to **FREEZE**. My belly feels sick, and I'm weak in the knees. I don't **FREEZE** like a statue or stand in one place, but I walk off the field with a very **RED** face.

Are you ever **EMBARRASSED?**

Do you want to **GO HOME?**

Do you ever wish people would **LEAVE YOU ALONE?**

Some of my friends **FLIP THEIR LIDS** at school.

When they feel big feelings... they lose their cool.

I don't **FLIP MY LID**, I don't **LOSE MY COOL,** because I'm good at hiding my feelings at school. I don't let them see it. I hold it all in, but when I get home, that's when it begins.

Some nights after school, I'm ready to **ROAR.**

I **RUN** straight to my room and I **SLAM** my door.

On other nights, I'm quiet and **SAD, CONFUSED**
or **UPSET, EMBARRASSED** or **MAD.**

My parents feel **WORRIED**, they don't know what to say when I'm in a **MOOD** after a **STRESSFUL** day.

They try to **HELP** me, They really do, but I still **FLIP MY LID**, I still **LOSE MY COOL.**

I really don't like **FLIPPING MY LID.**

I wish I could be a **CALM, COOL KID.**

Then one night mom and dad found a book.

We sat down together and started to look.

The book was **SUPER COOL** to me and
explained how to live together **MINDFULLY**.

One page taught us all about the **BRAIN** and how **STRESS** and **WORRY** can cause lots of **STRAIN**.

Another page taught us how to **BREATHE** so we don't lose our cool and **FIGHT, RUN,** or **FREEZE.**

The last page taught us a very fun game. It's called **MINDFUL GROUNDING**— That's really the name!

Here's how we do it,

Here's how it's done.

It all begins with **BREATH NUMBER ONE.**

BREATH ① SENSE OF SIGHT

We sit together with our eyes soft or closed, we breathe on purpose right through our nose. We notice our feet as they rest on the floor and wiggle our toes taking one breath more. Now we open our eyes and name five things we see, like a couch and a chair, book, clock, and TV.

BREATH ② SENSE OF HEARING

Again closing our eyes, we take our next breath and notice the rise and fall of our belly and chest. We open our eyes and name four things we hear. These sounds can be far away or they can be near. Is it a clock ticking softly or maybe the rain? We listen with ease, we don't need to strain.

BREATH ③ SENSE OF TOUCH

Again closing our eyes, we breathe a big breath and notice our hearts thumping strong in our chests. We open our eyes and touch three different things, like our pants, our shirt, or maybe a ring. We notice the textures. Are they soft or warm? What does it feel like? What is the form?

BREATH ④ SENSE OF SMELL

We return to our breathing, and we notice our breath. The game's almost over, we're doing our best. We open our eyes and name two things we smell. Is it pie in the oven or box of pastels?

BREATH ⑤ SENSE OF TASTE

We are almost finished, one more to go. We breathe deep breaths, nice and slow. We open our eyes and name one thing to eat. Is it sweet or sour? What's the name of your treat?

We sat very still and learned how to **BREATHE**, moving air in and out with a feeling of ease. With each breath we took, we counted to five and let the air out slowly while we closed our eyes.

MINDFUL GROUNDING can happen anytime, any place. It's a way to relax to stay connected and safe. Each night we do this after school, it helps us get centered and stay **CALM AND COOL.**

Remember some nights are tricky, and some nights are fun, but no matter what, we can choose not to run. We can choose not to **FIGHT** or **FLY** away too because grounding together keeps us **CALM AND COOL.**

WOULD YOUR FAMILY LIKE TO TRY IT TOO?

MINDFUL GROUNDING WITH THE SENSES

Invite your family to sit in a mindful body posture. Sit comfortably with your feet resting on the floor, your body tall and straight like a giraffe, your neck long, and your shoulders and face relaxed.

Begin to breathe in through your nose and out through your mouth, taking slow mindful breaths.

Your eyes can be closed or your lids softly relaxed.

Continue to breathe slow, deep breaths.

MINDFUL GROUNDING BREATH ① (SENSE OF SIGHT)

Breathe on purpose in through your nose, and on the next exhale, open your eyes and name five things you see. (You can choose to take turns telling one another, drawing the images, or keeping what you notice inside your own mind.)

MINDFUL GROUNDING BREATH ② (SENSE OF HEARING)

Breathe on purpose in through your nose, and on the next exhale, open your eyes and name four things you hear. (You can chose to take turns telling one another, drawing the images, or keeping what you notice inside your own mind.)

MINDFUL GROUNDING BREATH ③ (SENSE OF TOUCH)

Breathe on purpose in through your nose, and on the next exhale, open your eyes and name three things you feel. (You can chose to take turns telling one another, drawing the images, or keeping what you notice inside your own mind.)

MINDFUL GROUNDING BREATH (4) (SENSE OF SMELL)

Breathe on purpose in through your nose, and on the next exhale, open your eyes and name two things you smell. (You can chose to take turns telling one another, drawing the images, or keeping what you notice inside your own mind.)

MINDFUL GROUNDING BREATH (5) (SENSE OF TASTE)

Breathe on purpose in through your nose, and on the next exhale, open your eyes and name one thing you taste or enjoy eating. (You can chose to take turns telling one another, drawing the images, or keeping what you notice inside your own mind.)

GRATITUDE MOMENT:

Take a moment to continue to breathe slow, deep breaths and give gratitude to your senses.

You can say:

"Thank you eyes for helping me see all of the interesting sights of the world."

"Thank you ears for helping me hear all of the interesting sounds of the world."

"Thank you body for helping me touch all of the interesting textures of the world."

"Thank you nose for helping me smell all of the interesting smells of the world."

"Thank you mouth for helping me taste all of the interesting foods and drinks of the world."

Acknowledge how the mind, heart, and body feel after practicing mindful grounding of the senses:

"I FEEL WARM." "I FEEL SAFE." "I FEEL TIRED." "I FEEL CALM." "I FEEL PEACEFUL."

MINDFUL GROUNDING of the senses can be done anytime in your safe spaces.

NOTE TO FAMILIES, CAREGIVERS & EDUCATORS

Being a kid is tricky, and the rigor and demand for learning is real. Each child develops and navigates life at different rates and stages, depending upon the emotional and physical support each child has along the way.

I invite you to use this book as a starting point for conversations with your children as they begin to experience stress and anxious feelings.

Take the time to explore feelings and emotions with your children. Tell your children that all feelings are okay, but it's not a good idea to stay stuck in big emotions if that emotion doesn't help them to feel safe, connected, and loved. We are so much more than the sum of our emotions. We can become the boss of our emotions and not allow them to take control of our lives.

Talk to your children about feeling sad, upset, worried, or scared. Intentionally notice when these feelings surface, and teach your children how to manage their emotions rather than allowing their emotions to manage them.

One way to do this is through co-regulation. Children need our help regulating. Many dysregulated children don't regulate simply by being told to "calm down." There is much research showing that children who use mindfulness practices with supportive adults can learn self-regulation that may last a lifetime. A good investment I'd say.

Co-regulation is defined as "calming together." Brain science shows us that when children develop emotional self-regulation skills through consistent, calm, and loving caregivers, they are better able to handle life stress, control emotions, make responsible decisions, and show greater self-awareness. These skills are the foundation of human emotional intelligence, and it's our responsibility to teach these skills to our children.

May you and your children be forever well, safe, healthy, and happy as you calm the heart, mind, and body together.

Kellie Doyle Bailey, MA CCC-SLP, MMT /SELI,
Mindfulness & SEL Educator

ACKNOWLEDGMENTS

Shortly following the release of *Some Days I Flip My Lid* in October 2019, I received hundreds of requests for a sequel—one that depicted a main **character** who **might not** show externalizing behaviors at school, but once in the safety of home might **unravel in concerning ways** due to the stressors of being a kid—and Grace was born. My first book is loosely framed around **my** son who was often impacted by anxiety and demonstrated "lid flipping" dysregulating behaviors when he didn't feel safe and connected.

Some Nights I Flip My Lid is loosely framed around its illustrator and my daughter, Hannah Grace, who worked very hard to hold it together out in the world but often needed a bit more help (like many children) regulating at home. Our children benefited greatly from mindfulness practices, like grounding and breathing on purpose, to help regulate and find a sense of peace and calm.

Again, I'd like to give a nod of appreciation and gratitude to Dr. Dan Siegel for his work on lid flipping and the hand-brain model. For more information about Dr. Siegel's work, please visit www.drdansiegel.com.

AUTHOR

Siveleaf photography

KELLIE DOYLE BAILEY, MA CCC-SLP, MMT/SELI, is the proud mother of Hannah and Doyle Bailey who together were her best lid-flipping life teachers. She is a veteran speech language pathologist of 30 years, certified mindfulness educator, and social emotional learning instructor. She is the founder of Calm Cool Kids Educate and works in Maine helping educators, students, and families learn about mindfulness strategies to stay calm and cool. Kellie has a strong background in social emotional learning and the neurodevelopment of children and is deeply committed to sharing mindfulness and SEL strategies with everyone who loves children. Kellie teaches Mindfulness in Education at The University of Maine in Farmington. She lives on the coast of Maine with her husband Bruce, a lifelong Maine educator.

ILLUSTRATOR

Siveleaf photography

HANNAH G. BAILEY received a Bachelor of Arts degree from The University of Maine in Orono and is a middle school art teacher in Bucksport, ME. Hannah is pursuing a master's degree in school counseling when she isn't busy illustrating books. Her students love that she incorporates mindful breath breaks and grounding practices into her daily art instruction. She is a strong believer that all students require nurturing and emotional development to become optimal lifelong learners. Hannah lives on the coast of Maine.

DEDICATION

This book is dedicated to the thousands of children I have been blessed to learn from over the past 30 years in education and especially to my own children, Hannah and Doyle. Thank you for being my best life teachers. What a gift the children of the world are. May we each take still, small moments to truly see the needs of our small humans and work courageously to make every child feel safe, connected, and loved.

With so much gratitude, appreciation, and respect,

—Kellie Doyle Bailey